Fun
with
Science!

by Kelly Kong

PEARSON

Scott Foresman

Editorial Offices: Glenview, Illinois • Parsippany, New Jersey • New York, New York
Sales Offices: Needham, Massachusetts • Duluth, Georgia • Glenview, Illinois
Coppell, Texas • Ontario, California • Mesa, Arizona

ISBN: 0-328-13374-4

It's the weekend and you have finished your **chores.** What will you do with your free time? Maybe you will play a game or read a book. There are many ways to spend your **spare** time!

You probably have many hobbies. Some may take you outside. Others may involve friends or adults. One of your hobbies could even become your job one day! Did you know that many hobbies are related to science?

Zoology?

For example, do you enjoy taking care of animals? Scientists who study animals are called zoologists.

Archeology?

Do you like digging around in search of old objects? Archeologists are people who use clues found in today's world to study history and past cultures.

Astronomy?

Maybe you like watching the stars? An astronomer studies outer space.

Each of these hobbies is connected to science. Read on to find out more about the connections between hobbies and science!

A hummingbird is a tiny bird.

Learning from Animals

Have you ever spotted a bluebird flying across the sky? Have you ever seen a red cardinal sitting on a tree branch? Birds are incredible creatures. They come in many different shapes, sizes, and colors.

Birds can be tiny. Some hummingbirds are only two inches long! Other birds are much larger. Eagles have wingspans of almost eight feet! Birds can be very different from each other. A simple but powerful tool makes it easy to spot birds' differences.

5

The simple but powerful tool is a set of binoculars! Binoculars make faraway objects appear closer. With binoculars you can watch birds find food, eat, or care for their young.

Birds are often fearful of people. If you are farther away, it is less likely birds can hear or smell you. That means you are more likely to see the birds behave normally.

Watching birds and other animals is important. It helps zoologists understand more about their life cycles. By learning about animals' habits, zoologists can help them survive in their environments.

Use binoculars to watch birds without disturbing them.

Scarlet tanager

Flicker

Eastern bluebird

Digging Up the Past

Have you ever found old items in an **attic?** People sometimes like to save old items, such as **stamps** or an oil painting on an old **board.** Then they may sell them to **customers** at a yard sale.

Old and ancient items are found every day in many different places. When an ancient item is found, it often tells something about past peoples, cultures, and places.

It is fun to find old treasures from the past. Sometimes old items are **labeled.** Other times they are not. When items are not labeled and you do not know what they are, you can research the past to learn more about them!

You can learn about the past by talking to your family and neighbors, searching your attic, or going to the library and reading old newspapers.

Talk to a neighbor or visit your library for more information about the past.

Workers in China were digging a well to provide water for local people. As one worker dug, his shovel hit a hard object. He had hit a buried statue. Archeologists heard about the statue and visited the workers. When the archeologists dug deeper, they found a group of statues that were more than two thousand years old! Nobody had known that the statues existed. Archeologists researched the past to learn more about the treasured statues.

Before you start digging holes in search of lost treasures, however, it is important that you ask for permission from an adult. When you find something that is interesting, ask an adult to help you identify it.

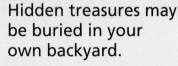

Hidden treasures may be buried in your own backyard.

These statues are treasures from the past!

Watching the Night Sky

Do you enjoy gazing up at a dark sky filled with twinkling stars? Stargazing is another popular hobby that relates to science. People have watched the stars in the night sky for thousands of years.

Saturn

Space has been called the final frontier. That is because it contains many mysteries and was difficult to study in the past.

Telescopes are tools that make observing space and the stars easier. Telescopes are made up of a set of lenses, mirrors, or both. They are used to make objects in the sky appear closer. You may use a small telescope when you stargaze.

Astronomers use huge, powerful telescopes to study planets and stars that are trillions of miles away. Astronomers have learned many things by watching the night sky.

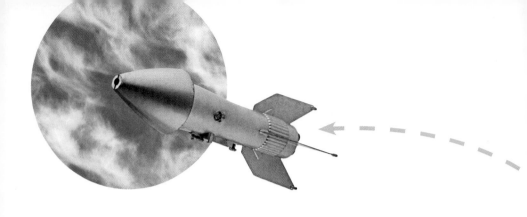

Fun with Hobbies

There are many other popular science hobbies out there. If you love animals, you can help take care of them. What you learn about animals now may help you become a veterinarian in the future! A veterinarian is a doctor who takes care of animals.

Caring for animals can be an interesting hobby!

As you have learned, many hobbies are related to science. And who knows? The science hobby that you start today could become your job in the future.

Science is a part of our daily lives. Turn your interests into hobbies to learn and have fun!

Hobbies are fun and can teach you a lot about science.

Glossary

attic *n.* the space in a house just below the roof and above the other rooms.

board *n.* a broad, thin piece of wood for use in building.

chores *n.* small tasks or easy jobs that you have to do regularly.

customers *n.* people who buy goods or services.

labeled *v.* to put or write a label on something.

spare *adj.* extra.

stamps *n.* small pieces of paper with glue on the back; postage stamps.